■SCHOLASTIC

Nonfiction
Read & Write Booklets
Human Body

by Alyse Sweeney

NEW YORK • TORONTO • LONDON • AUCKLAND • SYDNEY
MEXICO CITY • NEW DELHI • HONG KONG • BUENOS AIRES

Teaching
Resources

For Dad

Cover design by Brian LaRossa

Cover and interior illustrations by Maxie Chambliss

Interior design by Ellen Matlach for Boultinghouse & Boultinghouse, Inc.

ISBN-13: 978-0-439-56759-6

ISBN-10: 0-439-56759-9

Copyright © 2007 by Alyse Sweeney

Published by Scholastic Inc.

1 2 3 4 5 6 7 8 9 10   40   15 14 13 12 11 10 09 08 07

Contents

Nonfiction Read & Write Booklets

Introduction

During the time I was a Scholastic editor, a large part of my job was finding out from primary-grade teachers what materials would be most useful to them in the classroom. Over the years second- and third-grade teachers spoke of the growing need for the following:

- engaging nonfiction texts that tie in to the curriculum

- more opportunities to engage students in meaningful writing (including nonfiction writing)

- writing prompts that connect to texts and build higher-order thinking skills

Nonfiction Read & Write Booklets: Human Body delivers each of these valuable components in an interactive mini-book format. The ten booklets cover key topics about the human body and engage students with lively text, thought-provoking writing prompts, and opportunities to draw. Best of all, when students are finished, they'll have a unique, personalized book to take home and share. The sense of ownership and accomplishment that comes with completing these mini-books is highly motivating.

Each booklet is filled with a variety of nonfiction features and structures to help students learn to navigate informational text. They'll learn key concepts from reading charts, webs, and diagrams. In addition, each mini-book presents students with opportunities to write informational text. After reading a chart, diagram, or short passage, students are asked to infer, evaluate, apply, analyze, compare, explain, or summarize. As a result, children develop critical-thinking skills and gain a deeper understanding of each topic.

Once students have completed their booklets and shared them with classmates, encourage them to share their work with family members. When children share their writing with others, they gain confidence as writers and become more motivated to write. The repeated readings also help children develop fluency. Sending the books home provides families with opportunities to observe and support their children's literacy development as well as discover what topics they are learning about in school.

With these interactive booklets in hand, children reflect upon what they are reading, think critically, develop their own ideas, and express themselves in writing. Nonfiction Read & Write Booklets provide an engaging format for helping students comprehend the features of nonfiction and for satisfying their curiosity about the world around them.

Why Teach Nonfiction?

Research has provided insight into the importance of teaching nonfiction. Here are some key findings:

- Informational text helps students build knowledge of the world around them (e.g., Anderson & Guthrie, 1999; Duke & Kays, 1998, as cited in Duke & Bennett-Armistead, 2003). This can potentially deepen students' comprehension of subsequent texts (e.g., Wilson & Anderson, 1986, as cited in Duke & Bennett-Armistead, 2003).

- Many students struggle with content area reading (Vacca, 2002; Walpole, 1998, as cited in Kristo and Bamford, 2004). Providing students with high-quality nonfiction materials may help to better prepare them to meet these challenges.

- Studies have shown that some students prefer nonfiction to fiction (Donovan, Smolkin, and Lomax, 2000; Caswell and Duke, 1998, as cited in Boynton and Blevins, 2004). Including more nonfiction materials in your classroom instruction taps into these students' interests and may increase their level of motivation.

- Providing students in the lower grades with more exposure to nonfiction may alleviate the decline in achievement often observed in fourth grade (Chall, Jacobs, and Baldwin, 1990; Duke, 2000, as cited in Boynton and Blevins, 2005).

- Exposing students in the early grades to informational texts helps improve their skills as readers and writers of informational text when they are older (Papps, 1991; Sanacore, 1991, as cited in Kristo and Bamford, 2004).

- Teaching students to read nonfiction will give them real-world skills and prepare them for the materials they'll read outside of school. One study found that the text on the World Wide Web is 96 percent expository (Kamil & Lane, 1998, as cited in Duke & Bennett-Armistead, 2003). Students will encounter informational text not only on the Web but also all around them—it's essential that they have the tools to comprehend it.

Connections to the Standards

These books are designed to support you in meeting the following standards outlined by Mid-continent Research for Education and Learning (McREL), an organization that collects and synthesizes national and state standards.

Reading

—Uses the general skills and strategies of the reading process, including:

- Uses meaning clues such as picture captions, title, cover, and headings to aid comprehension.

—Uses reading skills and strategies to understand and interpret a variety of informational texts, including:

- Understands the main idea and supporting details of simple expository information.
- Relates new information to prior knowledge and experience.
- Uses text organizers (e.g., headings, topic and summary sentences, graphic features, typeface) to determine the main ideas and to locate information in a text.
- Understands structural patterns or organization in informational texts (e.g., chronological, logical, or sequential order; compare-and-contrast; cause-and-effect; proposition and support).

Writing

—Uses the general skills and strategies of the writing process.

—Uses the stylistic and rhetorical aspects of writing.

—Uses grammatical and mechanical conventions in written compositions.

Health

—Knows how to maintain and promote personal health.

- Knows basic personal hygiene habits required to maintain health.
- Understands the influence of rest, food choices, exercise, and sleep on a person's well-being.
- Knows the basic structure and functions of the human body systems.

—Understands essential concepts about nutrition and diet.

Source: *Content Knowledge: A Compendium of Standards and Benchmarks for K–12 Education.* 4th edition. (Mid-continent Research for Education and Learning, 2004)

How to Use This Book

These booklets can be completed during class or as homework. Before students begin, walk them through each page so that they clearly understand how to respond to the writing prompts and how to read any challenging text features, such as charts or diagrams. If students need additional support, guide them as they work on a section of a booklet. You might have students complete a booklet over the course of several days, working on a few pages at a time.

Activate Prior Knowledge

Introduce each booklet with a discussion that activates students' prior knowledge. Ask students what they know about the topic, what they think they'll learn about the topic from the booklet, and what they would like to learn about the topic.

Walk Through the Booklet

After introducing the booklet and discussing the topic, walk through the pages together to satisfy children's curiosity and clarify the instructions. Point out the writing and drawing prompts and explain to students that although everyone is starting with the same booklet, they will each have a unique book when they are finished.

Read, Write, Draw, and Learn

Read and discuss the text together, pointing out vocabulary words and raising questions. Then move on to the accompanying writing and drawing prompts. Generate possible answers with students. Encourage students to write in complete sentences. Talk about what they learned from a particular section. Were they surprised about something they learned? Do they want to know more about a topic?

Share

At various points in the bookmaking process, have students share their written responses with their classmates. Draw attention to the similarities and differences in their responses. Be sure to send the booklets home for students to share with families.

Extend Learning

On pages 7–8, you'll find two extension activities for each booklet. These will reinforce concepts covered in the books and explore a particular topic in more depth.

How to Assemble the Booklets

It works well to assemble the booklets together as a class.

Directions:

1. Carefully remove the perforated pages from the book.
2. Make double-sided copies of each page on standard 8½- by 11-inch paper.
3. Fold each page in half along the dashed line.
4. Place the pages in numerical order and staple along the spine.

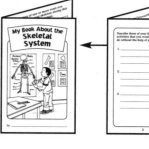

TIP: You may want to have students fill in their books before stapling them. This way the center pages will lie flat while students are writing.

Extension Activities

My Book About the Skeletal System

- Play the Boney-Hokey-Pokey! Students will love learning the names of bones with this clever song, found in *Bonz Inside-Out!* by Byron Glaser & Sandra Higashi (Harry N. Abrams, 2003).

- Discuss the difference between vertebrates and invertebrates. Then create a visual chart of vertebrates (such as humans, monkeys, birds, and frogs) and invertebrates (such as turtles, scorpions, lobsters, and beetles).

My Book About Muscles

- Create a three-way Venn diagram that compares three types of muscles. Have students refer to the chart on page 1 of the booklet and place various pieces of information on the Venn diagram.

- Create a muscle movement chart. Have students share their list of activities that the flexors, orbicularis oris, and soleus muscles allow them to do (page 4 of the booklet). Record the responses on a chart. A wide variety of answers may coincide with the wide variety of movements for each muscle. Brainstorm additional activities if necessary. Invite students to add more muscles to the chart for further exploration.

My Book About the Heart and Circulation

- Have students stand still and feel their own heartbeat. Then have them do ten jumping jacks and feel their heartbeat again. What did they notice? Discuss the results. Explain that their bodies need more oxygen when they exercise. The heart pumps faster so that it can deliver more blood and oxygen to the muscles.

- Fill one-quart jars with water to compare how much blood is in each of the following: a baby (one quart), a child (three quarts), and an adult (five quarts). If you don't have jars, simply create a visual chart or a pictograph with this information.

My Book About the Brain and Nervous System

- How heavy does a three-pound brain feel? Bring in a variety of fruits and vegetables and a scale. Have volunteers add and subtract items to and from the scale until they get to three pounds.

- Invite students to write about a favorite memory. Remind them that the brain stores our memories. Allow time for students to share their memories with the class.

My Book About the Digestive System

- Use various forms of measurement to demonstrate the length of the small intestines (13–16 feet) and large intestines (five feet). For example, you might have students cut lengths of string or line up books or other objects to show these lengths. Create a chart depicting the results.

- Show how the esophagus works. Squeeze a new tube of toothpaste over a plate to show how the esophagus squeezes its muscular walls to push food down into the stomach.

My Book About the Respiratory System

- Compare the temperature of inhaled air and exhaled air. Have students take a deep breath and blow the air into their cupped hands. Can students explain why the air they exhaled is warmer than the air they inhaled?

- Use the information presented on page 6 of the booklet to create a breathing chart. Label the rows "Breathe In" and "Breathe Out." Label the columns "Rib Cage" and "Diaphragm." Invite students to refer to page 6 of their booklets and provide the correct information for each box.

My Book About the Five Senses

- To make students more aware of their senses, create a class senses chart for students to fill in over the course of several days. On one axis of the chart, write each child's name. On the other axis, write each of the five senses. Students fill in the chart with objects around the classroom that they see, hear, feel, taste, and smell.

- Create a five senses bulletin board. Compile students' responses from the writing exercise on page 2. Have students share their responses, one sense at a time, while you record them on a large sheet of chart paper. When responses for all five senses have been recorded, transfer the pages to a bulletin board. Invite students to draw pictures that accompany the responses.

My Book About Teeth

- Have students write about the first time they lost a tooth. Where were they? How did they feel? How did family members react? Invite students to share their stories with one another and compare experiences.

- Have students choose an animal whose teeth they would like to research. How are the animal's teeth similar to and different from their own? Students can present the information on a chart or Venn diagram.

My Book About Skin

- Ask students to study the ridges on their fingers that make fingerprints. Do they know what the ridges are for? Record their responses on a chart. Then hand out two pieces of tape each to students and ask them to wrap the tape around the thumb and index finger of the same hand. Place a plastic chip or coin on the desk in front of each child. Invite students to pick up the object with their tape-covered fingers. Ask if it is harder or easier to pick up the object with the taped fingers. Have students take off the tape to pick up the object and compare the experiences.

- Convert a Venn diagram to a paragraph. On chart paper or an overhead transparency, do a think-aloud as you convert the information on the Venn diagram on page 6 of the booklet to a paragraph.

My Book About Staying Healthy

- Have students keep a health journal for a week. Invite students to think and write about the ways that they care for their bodies and stay healthy each day. Encourage students to notice ways they can replace unhealthy habits with healthy ones.

- Create healthy-habit advertisements. Divide the class into five groups and assign each group one healthy habit, such as drinking water, washing hands, or getting a good night's sleep. Have students work together to create a poster that advertises the habit and explains why it's important.

Selected References

Boynton, A. & Blevins, W. (2005). *Nonfiction passages with graphic organizers for independent practice: Grades 2–4*. New York: Scholastic.

Boynton, A. & Blevins, W. (2004). *Teaching students to read nonfiction: Grades 2–4*. New York: Scholastic.

Duke, N. K., & Bennett-Armistead, S. V. (2003). *Reading & writing informational text in the primary grades*. New York: Scholastic.

Kristo, J. V., & Bamford, R. A. (2004). *Nonfiction in focus*. New York: Scholastic.

My Book About the Skeletal System

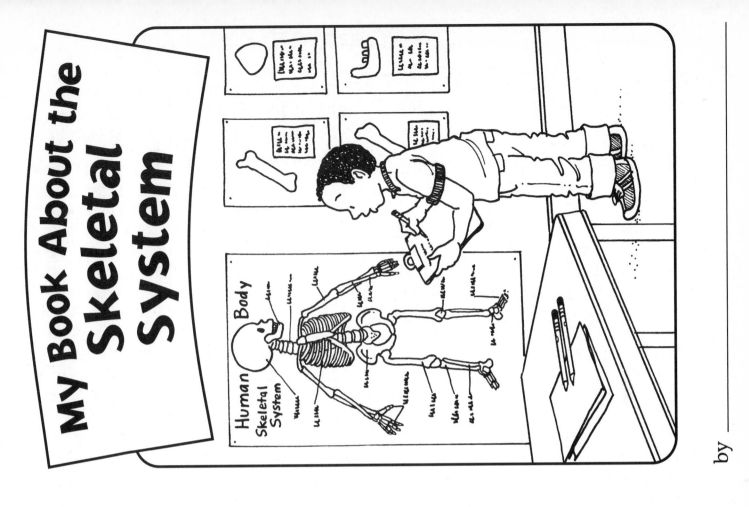

Bones of All Shapes and Sizes

Your skeleton is made up of:

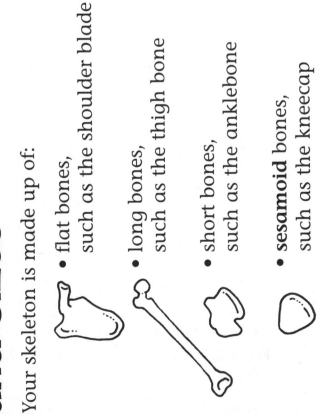

- flat bones, such as the shoulder blade

- long bones, such as the thigh bone

- short bones, such as the anklebone

- **sesamoid** bones, such as the kneecap

- irregular bones, such as **vertebrae**

Why do you think a skeleton needs bones of different shapes and sizes?

_____

_____

_____

7

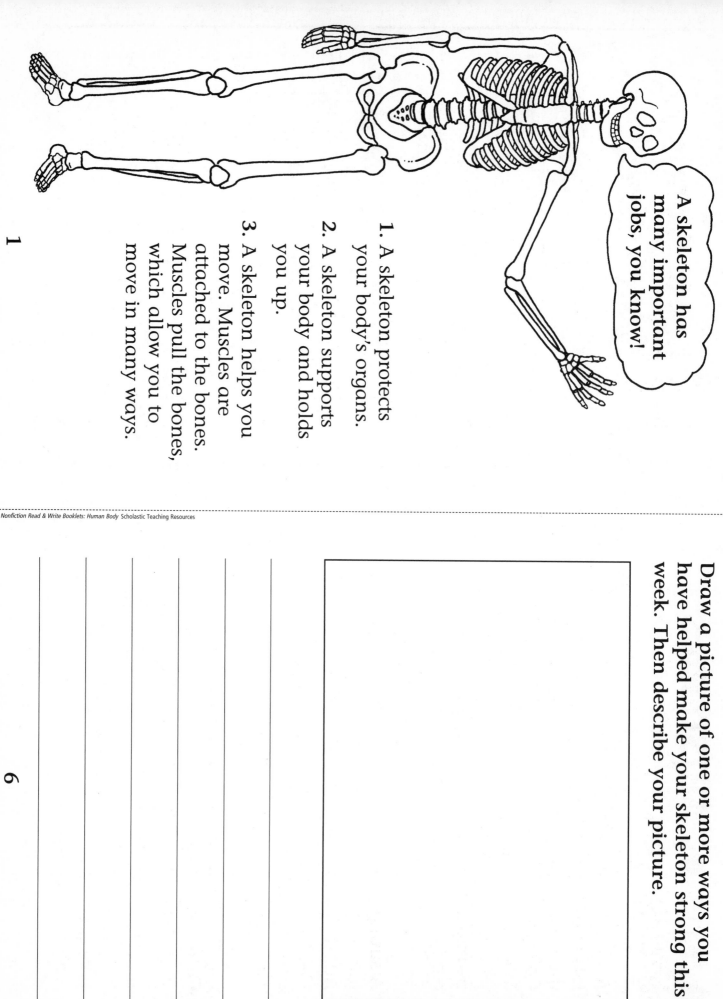

A skeleton has many important jobs, you know!

1. A skeleton protects your body's organs.
2. A skeleton supports your body and holds you up.
3. A skeleton helps you move. Muscles are attached to the bones. Muscles pull the bones, which allow you to move in many ways.

1

Draw a picture of one or more ways you have helped make your skeleton strong this week. Then describe your picture.

6

Describe three of your favorite activities that you would not be able to do without the help of your skeleton.

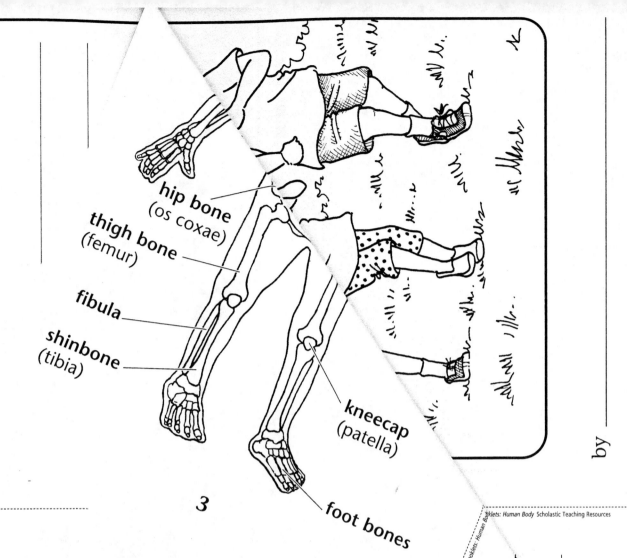

hip bone
(os coxae)

thigh bone
(femur)

fibula

shinbone
(tibia)

kneecap
(patella)

foot bones

3

by _____

A Strong Skeleton Needs . . .

- A strong skeleton needs lots of calcium to keep the bones strong. Calcium is found in foods such as milk, yogurt, cheese, broccoli, beans, oranges, and canned sardines.

- A strong skeleton needs lots of exercise, such as running and jumping. Exercise makes bones strong and helps joints move easily.

- A strong skeleton needs its owner to learn how to prevent injuries like broken bones. Wear a helmet when you ride a bike and protective gear when you play sports.

5

Describe three of your favorite activities that you would not be able to do without the help of your skeleton.

1. _____

_____

_____

2. _____

_____

_____

3. _____

_____

_____

2

A Strong Skeleton Needs . . .

- A strong skeleton needs lots of calcium to keep the bones strong. Calcium is found in foods such as milk, yogurt, cheese, broccoli, beans, oranges, and canned sardines.

- A strong skeleton needs lots of exercise, such as running and jumping. Exercise makes bones strong and helps joints move easily.

- A strong skeleton needs its owner to learn how to prevent injuries like broken bones. Wear a helmet when you ride a bike and protective gear when you play sports.

5

Your Skeleton

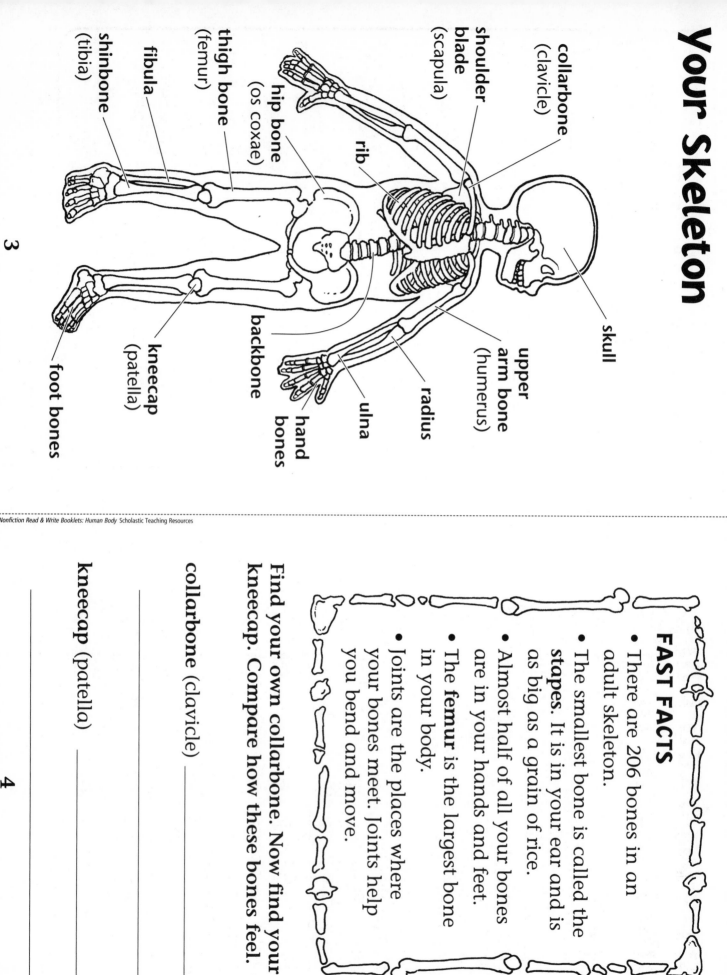

collarbone
(clavicle)

shoulder
blade
(scapula)

rib

hip bone
(os coxae)

thigh bone
(femur)

fibula

shinbone
(tibia)

backbone

kneecap
(patella)

foot bones

skull

upper
arm bone
(humerus)

radius

ulna

hand
bones

Nonfiction Read & Write Booklets: Human Body Scholastic Teaching Resources

FAST FACTS

- There are 206 bones in an adult skeleton.

- The smallest bone is called the **stapes**. It is in your ear and is as big as a grain of rice.

- Almost half of all your bones are in your hands and feet.

- The **femur** is the largest bone in your body.

- Joints are the places where your bones meet. Joints help you bend and move.

Find your own collarbone. Now find your kneecap. Compare how these bones feel.

collarbone (clavicle) _____

kneecap (patella) _____

My Book About Muscles

by _____

Three Ways to Keep Your Muscles Healthy

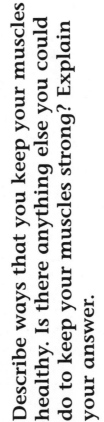

1. Eat foods with lots of protein, like meat, fish, eggs, milk, and beans. High-protein foods help build and repair muscle.

2. Exercise regularly to keep muscles strong.

3. Warm up your muscles before you play a sport. Warm-up exercises and stretching help prevent muscle strains and pulls.

Describe ways that you keep your muscles healthy. Is there anything else you could do to keep your muscles strong? Explain your answer.

_____

_____

_____

7

Move It!

Thanks to our muscles, we can move our bodies in hundreds of ways. Some muscles cover our skeleton. Other muscles are found in parts of our body, like our heart and intestines.

THREE TYPES OF MUSCLES

skeletal muscle	Skeletal muscles hold your bones together and move your skeleton. These are the muscles that allow you to jump, smile, and hold a pencil. These are the muscles that you control.
smooth muscle	Smooth muscles are found in organs such as your intestines. These muscles move automatically. This means they move without your thinking about it.
cardiac muscle	Cardiac muscle is found only in your heart. It tightens and relaxes about 70 to 100 times per minute, causing your heart to pump blood. This muscle also moves automatically.

1

I feel _____
(emotion)

when _____
(situation)

I feel _____
(emotion)

when _____
(situation)

I feel _____
(emotion)

when _____
(situation)

6

Voluntary muscles are muscles that you control. Skeletal muscle falls under this category.

Involuntary muscles are muscles that move without your thinking about it. Smooth muscle and cardiac muscle fall under this category.

How would our lives be different if we controlled our smooth and cardiac muscles the way we control our skeletal muscles?

_____

_____

_____

_____

_____

_____

2

Muscles Help You Express Yourself!

You have more than 40 muscles in your face. These muscles allow you to show many different facial expressions. Facial expressions help us show our emotions, or feelings.

Use your face muscles to make the same expression as each face shown. Then complete each sentence.

Write a word that best describes the emotion being expressed. Then describe a situation that makes you feel that emotion.

I feel _____
      (emotion)

when _____
      (situation)

5

Skeletal Muscles

You have more than 600 skeletal muscles in your body. This diagram shows some of the main muscles and how they help you move.

trapezius
moves
neck

deltoid
raises
shoulders

triceps
straightens
arm

biceps
bends arm

quadriceps
straightens leg

gastrocnemius
bends knee
and lifts heel

soleus
pulls up ankle

frontalis
raises eyebrows

orbicularis oculi
raises eyelid

orbicularis oris
moves lips

pectoralis major
rotates arm

flexors
bend wrist
and fingers

rectus abdominis
pulls in abdomen

adductor magnus
moves upper leg
to the side

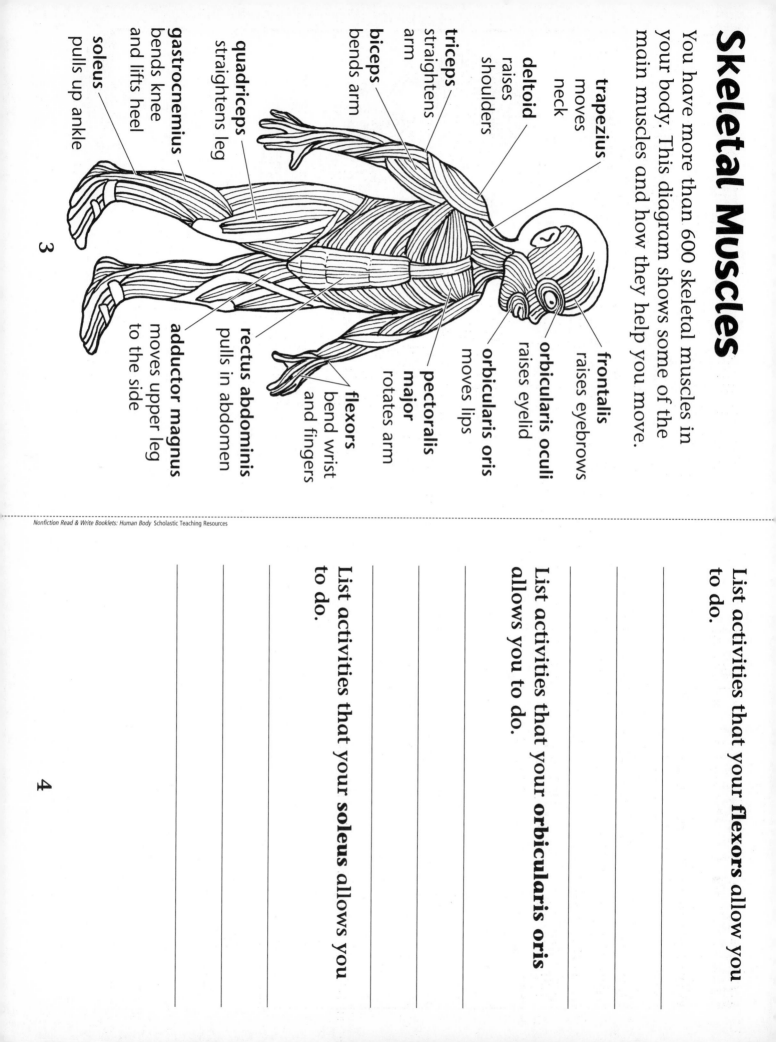

3

List activities that your **flexors** allow you to do.

_____

_____

_____

List activities that your **orbicularis oris** allows you to do.

_____

_____

_____

List activities that your **soleus** allows you to do.

_____

_____

_____

4

My Book About the Heart and Circulation

by _____

Have a Healthy Heart

When you are active, you are exercising your heart muscle and making it strong.

Draw a picture that shows you doing your favorite physical activity or a physical activity that you would like to try. Then describe what is happening in your picture.

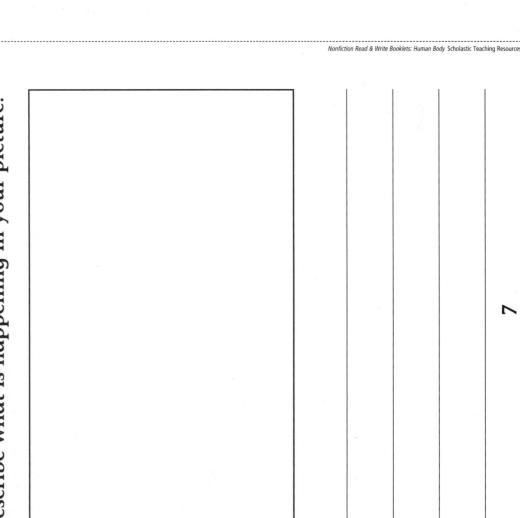

_____

_____

_____

7

Your Hardworking Heart

Your heart is a strong muscle that pumps blood to the rest of your body. It never gets tired!

Your heart pumps, or beats, about 70 to 100 times per minute when you are relaxed. When you are excited, scared, or exercising, your heart beats up to about 200 times per minute.

This hardworking muscle is about the size of your fist.

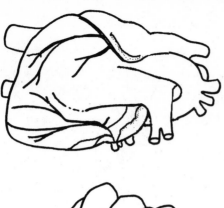

Nonfiction Read & Write Booklets: Human Body Scholastic Teaching Resources

Describe a time when you got a cut.

_____

_____

Which part of the blood helped you stop bleeding?

_____

_____

Describe how you feel when you are sick with a cold.

_____

_____

Which part of the blood helps you fight cold germs?

_____

_____

Describe three times when your heart rate went way up. Were you frightened? Happy? Playing a sport?

1. _____

_____

_____

2. _____

_____

_____

3. _____

_____

_____

2

What's in a Drop of Blood?

white blood cells, which fight germs.

platelets, which stop cuts from bleeding too much.

Each drop of blood has . . .

red blood cells, which carry oxygen.

plasma, which is a yellowish liquid made mostly of water.

5

A Powerful Pump

Your heart pumps blood to all parts of your body. The blood travels through blood vessels called **arteries** and **veins**. Blood has the important job of bringing **oxygen** and food to all your body parts. Blood also carries away waste.

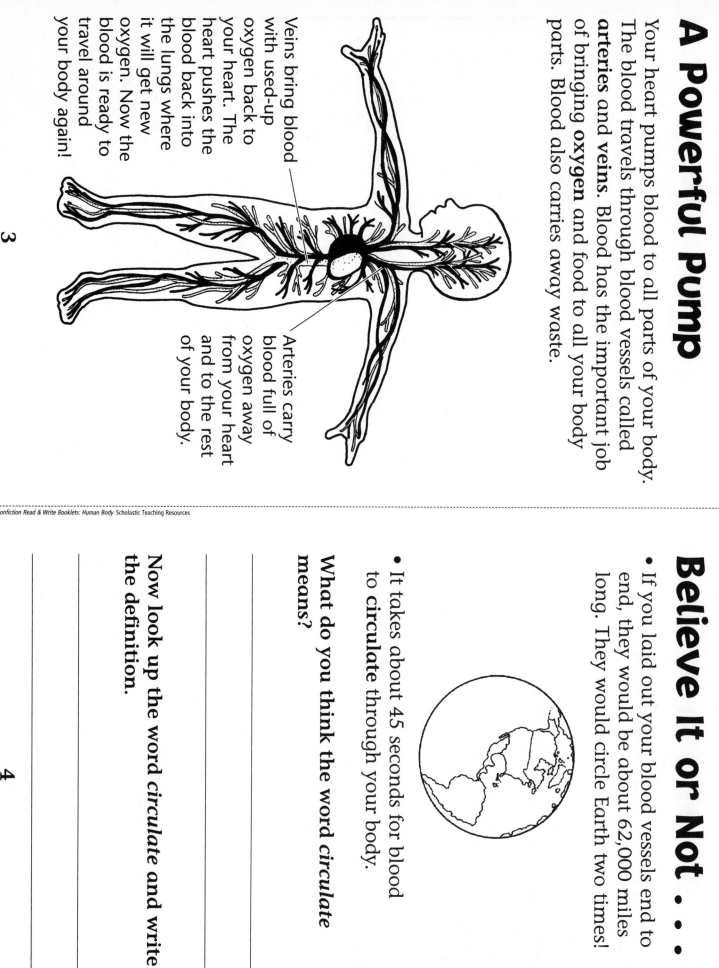

Veins bring blood with used-up oxygen back to your heart. The heart pushes the blood back into the lungs where it will get new oxygen. Now the blood is ready to travel around your body again!

Arteries carry blood full of oxygen away from your heart and to the rest of your body.

3

Believe It or Not . . .

- If you laid out your blood vessels end to end, they would be about 62,000 miles long. They would circle Earth two times!

- It takes about 45 seconds for blood to circulate through your body.

What do you think the word *circulate* means?

_____

_____

Now look up the word *circulate* and write the definition.

_____

_____

_____

4

My Book About the Brain and Nervous System

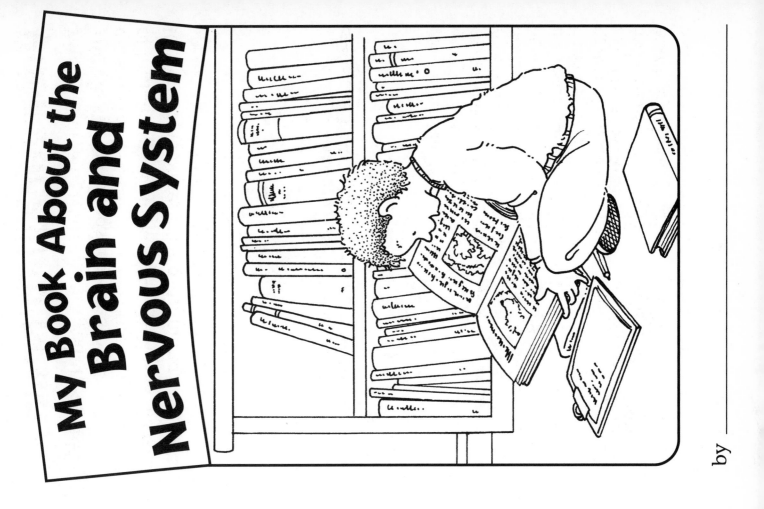

by _____

Play It Safe!

Your skull acts like a hard helmet and protects the soft brain inside. However, it is still important to wear a helmet when you ride a bike or scooter or do other activities.

Imagine you have a friend who does not want to wear a helmet when he or she rides a bike. Write a letter explaining why it's important to wear a helmet.

Dear _____,

_____

_____

_____

_____

Your friend,

_____

7

Your Amazing Brain

Your brain controls everything you think, feel, and do. The brain has three main parts.

The **cerebrum** is the largest part of the brain. It controls activities such as thinking, speaking, hearing, and smelling.

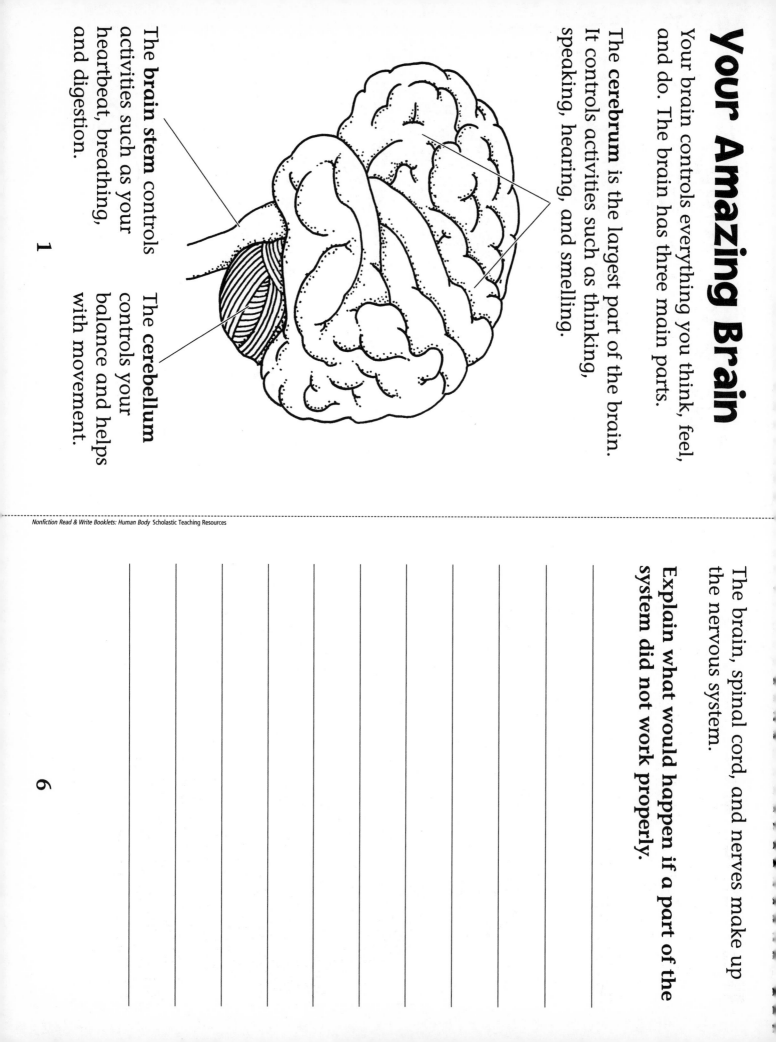

The **brain stem** controls activities such as your heartbeat, breathing, and digestion.

The **cerebellum** controls your balance and helps with movement.

Nonfiction Read & Write Booklets: Human Body Scholastic Teaching Resources

The brain, spinal cord, and nerves make up the nervous system.

Explain what would happen if a part of the system did not work properly.

Words and Phrases That Describe the Brain

soft   grayish pink

wrinkled like a walnut shell

weighs about three pounds (for an adult)

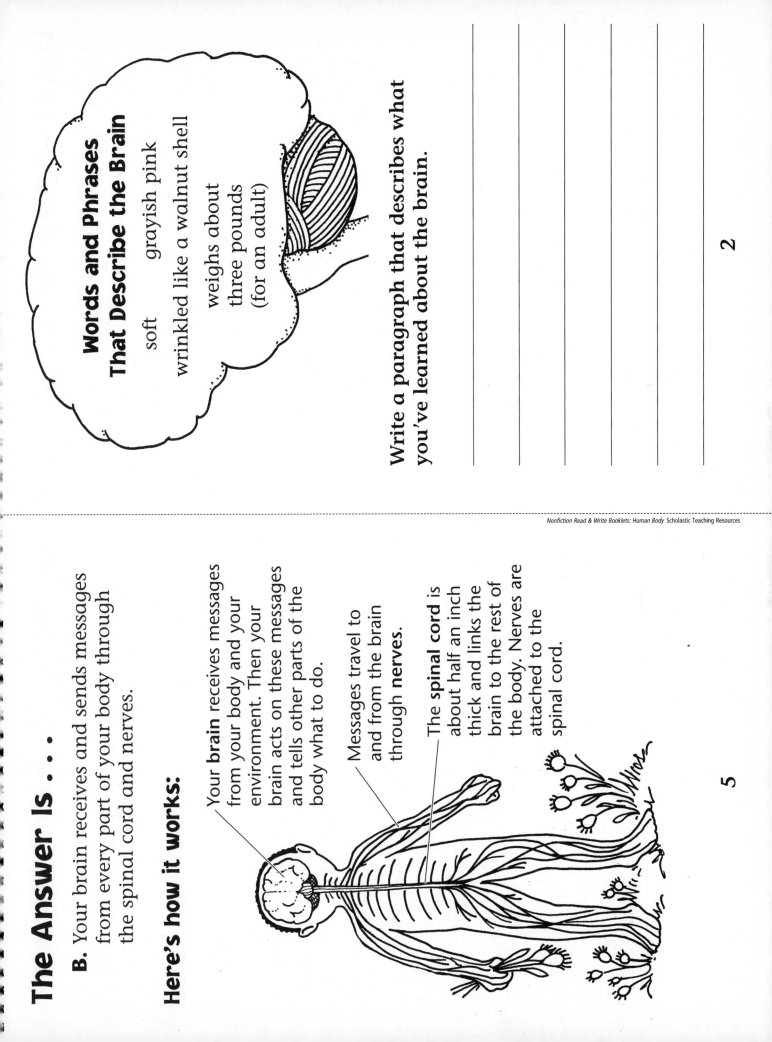

Write a paragraph that describes what you've learned about the brain.

2

The Answer Is . . .

B. Your brain receives and sends messages from every part of your body through the spinal cord and nerves.

Here's how it works:

Your **brain** receives messages from your body and your environment. Then your brain acts on these messages and tells other parts of the body what to do.

Messages travel to and from the brain through **nerves.**

The **spinal cord** is about half an inch thick and links the brain to the rest of the body. Nerves are attached to the spinal cord.

5

A Closer Look at the Cerebrum

The outer layer of the cerebrum is called the cerebral cortex. Different parts of the cerebral cortex do different jobs. Scientists have labeled these areas on a brain map.

hearing

smell

speech

movement

touch

taste

sight

Nonfiction Read & Write Booklets: Human Body Scholastic Teaching Resources

Think!

How do you think your brain communicates with your arm when you want to throw a ball? Or with your mouth when you want to speak?

A. It's magic! Your body just knows what to do.

B. Your brain receives and sends messages from every part of your body through the spinal cord and nerves.

C. Your brain is attached to your skull, and your skull communicates with the rest of your body.

Which answer do you think is correct?

Why? _____

_____

_____

_____

_____

My Book About the Digestive System

by _____

Feed Me Fiber!

You learned on page 5 that fiber helps the muscles in your intestines work better—which helps your digestive system work properly. Fiber is found in foods like beans, whole wheat bread, whole wheat pasta, apples, strawberries, cherries, some cereals, cauliflower, broccoli, and green beans.

Draw a fiber-rich meal. Then describe what foods you included in your drawing.

7

Feeding Your Body

Your body needs food to survive.

• Food gives you energy.
• Food allows you to grow.
• Food gives your body the fat it needs to keep you warm.

Before the food can do any of these jobs, your body has to break it down into smaller pieces. Once it has done so, the nutrients from the food can get into your blood, and your body can use them. This process of breaking down food is called **digestion**.

Nonfiction Read & Write Booklets: Human Body Scholastic Teaching Resources

What is the best way to get a good balance of nutrients and fiber in your diet?

_____

_____

_____

_____

Why is it important to eat a good balance of foods?

_____

_____

_____

_____

_____

_____

The digestive system includes four body parts:

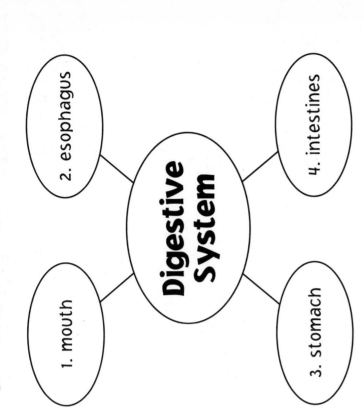

- Digestive System
  - 1. mouth
  - 2. esophagus
  - 3. stomach
  - 4. intestines

In which body part do you think digestion begins? Explain your answer.

_____

_____

_____

_____

2

Nonfiction Read & Write Booklets: Human Body Scholastic Teaching Resources

A Good, Balanced Diet

Our bodies get fiber and nutrients from food.

Name	Where It Is Found	What It Does
fiber	whole wheat bread, fruits, vegetables	helps the muscles in your intestines work better
protein	fish, meat, eggs	helps your body grow and repair itself
carbo-hydrates	pasta, breads, beans	give your body energy
fats	cheese, nuts, fish	give your body energy and help keep you warm
vitamins	fruits, vegetables	help your cells work well
minerals	fruits, vegetables, milk	help your cells work well
water	water, other liquids, food	carries nutrients into cells and keeps your body cool when you sweat

5

Digestion Begins in the Mouth!

1. In the **mouth**, teeth tear and chew the food. Saliva softens the food, making it easier to chew and swallow. The tongue helps push the food down the throat to the esophagus.

2. The **esophagus** is a muscular tube that squeezes food down into the stomach.

3. The strong walls of the **stomach** squeeze to mix the food with digestive juices. After a few hours, the chunks of food turn into a thick liquid called **chyme**.

Describe what happened to the breakfast, lunch, or snack that you ate today.

4. Every few minutes, the stomach lets out small amounts of chyme into the **small intestine**. Digestion is completed here. The parts of the food that the body can use move into the bloodstream.

5. The parts of the food that the body cannot use are called waste. Waste is stored at the end of the **large intestine**. It passes out of the body when you use the bathroom.

3

4

My Book About the Respiratory System

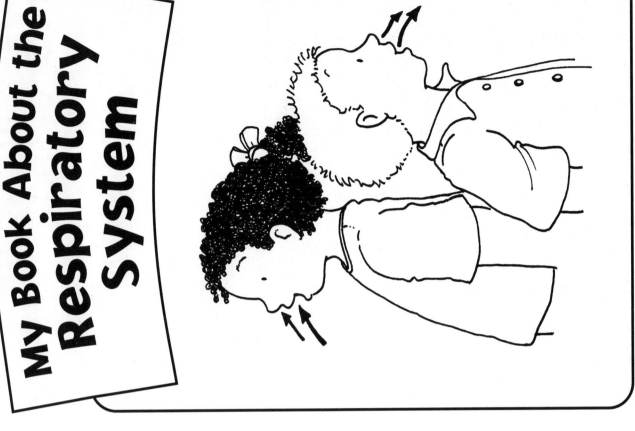

by _____

Breathe Hard!

You breathe harder and faster when you are active. That's because your muscles start to run low on oxygen. Hard, fast breathing quickly gets oxygen to your muscles.

Draw a picture that shows you being active. Describe your picture and the way your body feels when you do this activity.

_____

_____

_____

7

What's in the Air We Breathe?

Oxygen! Oxygen is a gas in the air that your body needs to live. Your body uses oxygen to turn food into energy. Every time you breathe in, you bring oxygen into your body. Every time you breathe out, you get rid of a waste gas called **carbon dioxide**. This process is called respiration.

Breathe In

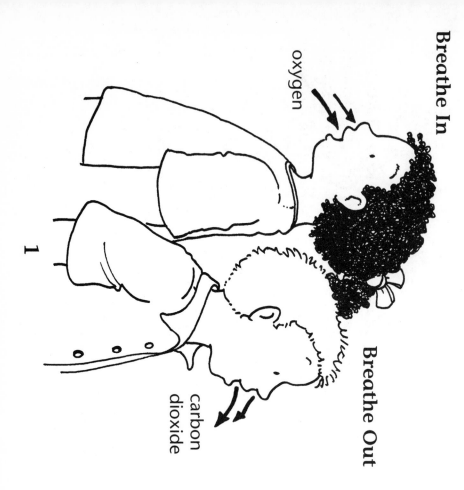

oxygen

carbon dioxide

Breathe Out

1

Here's How It Works:

Breathing In	Breathing Out
Your diaphragm moves down.	Your diaphragm moves upward.
Your rib cage moves upward and outward.	Your rib cage moves downward and inward.
Now there is lots of room for the lungs to fill with air.	Now there is less room in the chest, and air is squeezed out of the lungs.

6

Put your hands on your stomach and take a deep breath. Describe what your stomach does when you breathe in. Then explain what makes this happen.

_____

_____

_____

_____

_____

Put your hands on your stomach, take a deep breath, and then breathe out. Describe what your stomach does when you breathe out. Then explain what makes this happen.

_____

_____

_____

_____

_____

2

The Muscles Behind Breathing

Lungs are not made of muscle. They are delicate and spongy. They need the strong **diaphragm** and rib muscles to make breathing possible. The diaphragm is below the lungs. The rib cage surrounds the lungs.

lungs

ribs

diaphragm

5

How Do We Breathe?

The respiratory system includes the lungs, air passages, and breathing muscles. Read the diagram to learn how air travels through your body.

1. Air enters your nose and mouth. Inside the **nasal cavity**, the air is warmed, cleaned, and moistened.

2. The air moves down the windpipe, or **trachea.**

3. The air arrives in the **lungs.** Blood in your lungs picks up the oxygen and carries it to the rest of your body.

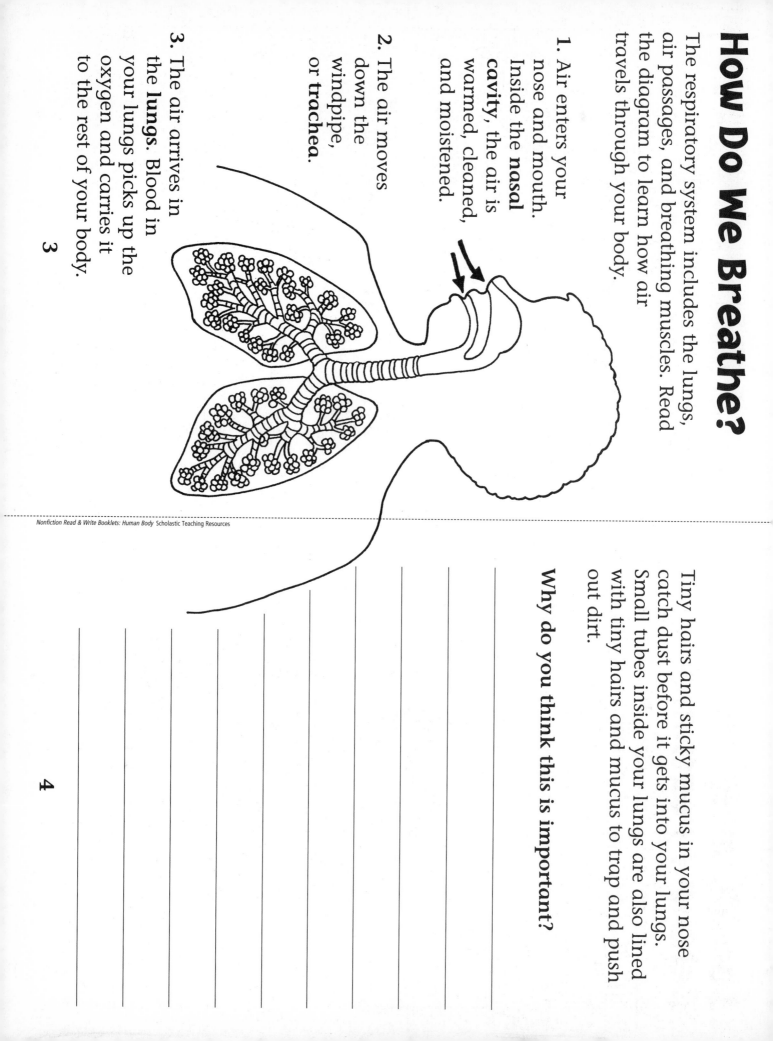

Tiny hairs and sticky mucus in your nose catch dust before it gets into your lungs. Small tubes inside your lungs are also lined with tiny hairs and mucus to trap and push out dirt.

Why do you think this is important?

_____

_____

_____

_____

_____

_____

_____

Nonfiction Read & Write Booklets: Human Body Scholastic Teaching Resources

My Book About the Five Senses

by _____

Senses at Work

Think about an activity that you love to do, such as drawing, riding your bike, or playing a sport. Draw a picture that shows you doing that activity. Then describe how you use your senses when you do the activity. How many senses do you use?

7

The Five Senses

Our senses allow us to see our friends, hear a guitar, smell cookies baking, taste a crisp apple, and feel a warm breeze. What makes this possible? Our sense organs: the eyes, ears, nose, tongue, and skin. Each sense organ sends messages about the world to our brain with special nerve cells called **receptors**.

Where are the receptors for each sense?

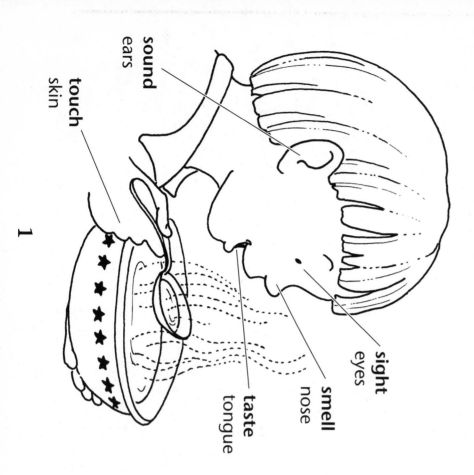

sight
eyes

smell
nose

taste
tongue

sound
ears

touch
skin

1

Nonfiction Read & Write Booklets: Human Body Scholastic Teaching Resources

---

Taste buds are not the tiny bumps you can see on your tongue. Those are called **papillae**. Taste buds are mostly found on the papillae but are too small to see. The tongue has about 10,000 taste buds.

Skin is the largest organ.

Which fact or facts did you find most interesting? Why?

6

I use my eyes to . . .

_____
_____
_____

I use my ears to . . .

_____
_____
_____

I use my nose to . . .

_____
_____
_____

I use my tongue to . . .

_____
_____
_____

I use my skin to . . .

_____
_____
_____

2

Did You Know . . . ?

Most of the eyeball is hidden in your skull.

As you get older, your sense of smell gets worse.

The ear cleans itself. Sticky wax inside the ear traps dirt. When the wax dries up, it moves to the outside of your ear and falls out. Your ear is always making more wax.

5

How the Senses Work

sight	You see something when light bounces off an object and back to your eyes. Receptors react to the light and send an image to the brain.
hearing	You hear a sound when vibrations in the air travel deep into your ear. The vibrations cause the liquid in the inner ear to move, which makes tiny hairs move. This movement sends signals to the brain.
smell	You smell something when tiny particles in the air enter your nose. Deep in the nose, receptors send a message about the odor to the brain.
taste	You taste when food dissolved in saliva passes over the taste buds on your tongue. Receptors send messages about the taste to the brain.
touch	You have receptors in the skin that detect sensations such as temperature, pain, and pressure. These receptors send messages to the brain about what you feel.

3

Nonfiction Read & Write Booklets: Human Body Scholastic Teaching Resources

Does the brain play a small role or big role in how you see, hear, smell, taste, and feel things?

_____

_____

Explain your answer.

_____

_____

_____

_____

_____

_____

_____

_____

4

My Book About Teeth

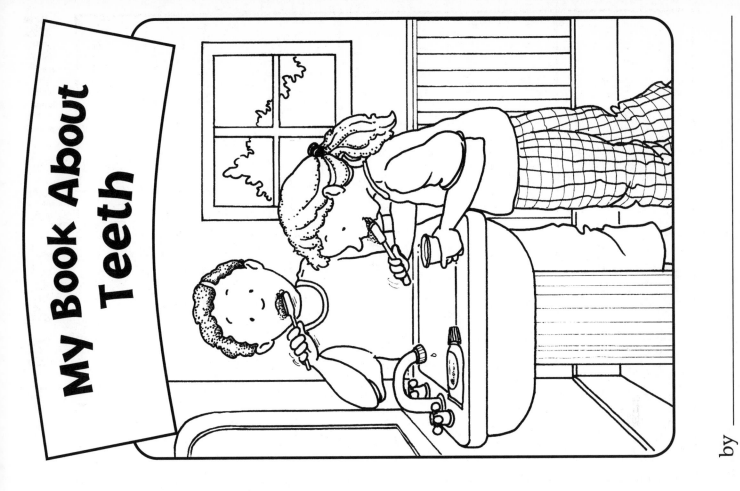

by _____

Caring for Your Teeth

1. Brush your teeth at least twice a day.

2. Floss to remove food that's stuck between your teeth.

3. Eat healthy foods.

4. Go to the dentist for checkups and cleanings.

Look at your smile in the mirror. Then draw a picture of your smile in the mirror below.

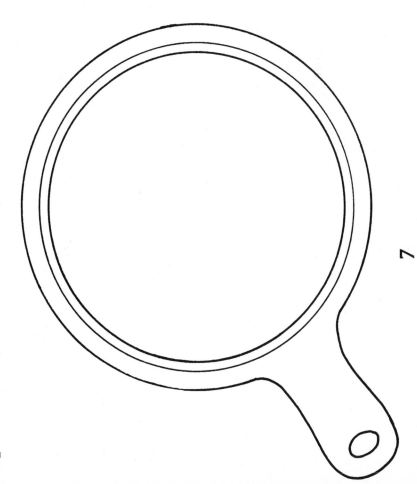

7

Thank You, Teeth!

What do your teeth do? Read the web below to find out.

They help give your face its shape.

Teeth

They help you bite and chew food.

They help you say certain sounds (like the **th** sound in **teeth**).

Nonfiction Read & Write Booklets: Human Body Scholastic Teaching Resources

---

Why do we have different kinds of teeth?

_____

_____

_____

_____

Explain why it would be difficult to eat a piece of pizza without your incisors.

_____

_____

_____

_____

_____

_____

_____

_____

Your Changing Mouth

Babies are born without teeth. By six or seven months, **primary teeth** (also called baby teeth) begin to come in. All 20 baby teeth are in by age 3.

Between ages 5 and 7, the baby teeth begin to fall out, one by one. The baby teeth are pushed out of the way by your **permanent teeth**.

By about age 14, you will have your full set of permanent teeth—28 in all.

Beginning at age 16, four **wisdom teeth** come in. These are the teeth in the very back of your mouth.

How many teeth have you lost so far? _____

2

Different Teeth for Different Jobs

incisors
canines
premolars
molars

TYPES OF PERMANENT TEETH

incisors	These teeth have sharp, flat ends for slicing through food when you bite.
canines	These sharp, pointy teeth help you grip and tear food.
premolars	Premolars have ridges for crushing and grinding food.
molars	Molars are the strongest teeth. They are wider and stronger and have more ridges than premolars.

5

What's in a Tooth?

Enamel is a hard and shiny substance that covers the crown and protects the tooth.

The **crown** is the part of the tooth you can see above the gum.

The **pulp** is where the nerve endings and blood vessels are found.

The **root** is the part of the tooth below the gum.

Nerves send messages to the brain about what the tooth is feeling.

Dentin is a hard material that makes up much of the tooth. It protects the pulp in the center of the tooth.

Blood vessels bring nutrients to the tooth and keep it healthy.

The **jawbone** is where the root of the tooth is held in place.

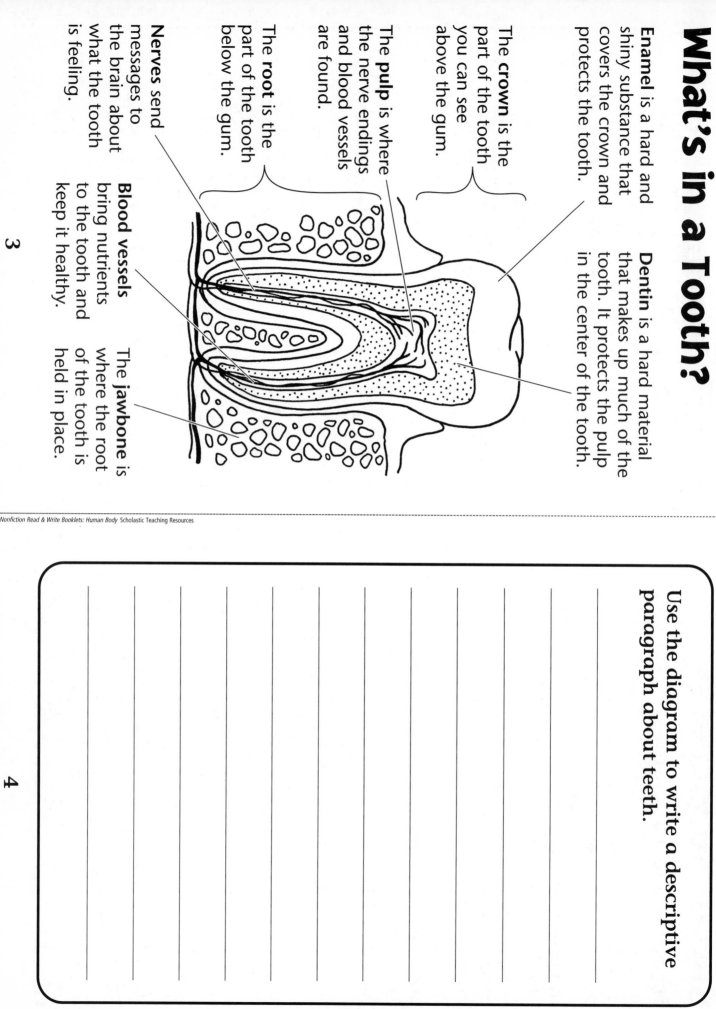

3

Nonfiction Read & Write Booklets: Human Body Scholastic Teaching Resources

Use the diagram to write a descriptive paragraph about teeth.

4

My Book About Skin

by _____

Super Sunscreen

The best way to care for your skin is to wear sunscreen. Sunscreen actually helps block the harmful rays of the sun from burning and damaging your skin.

Imagine you created a new brand of sunscreen. Give it a name and write an advertisement for your sunscreen. Describe its color, smell, and protective powers. Then draw a label for the bottle.

7

Six Super Ways Skin Protects You

1 Skin protects the body from outside germs.

2 Skin is waterproof and stops water from soaking into the body.

3 Skin helps control your body temperature.

4 Skin produces **melanin**, which protects skin cells from harmful sun rays.

5 Skin allows you to feel sensations such as heat, coolness, smoothness, roughness, softness, and hardness.

6 Skin protects your inside organs from outside elements.

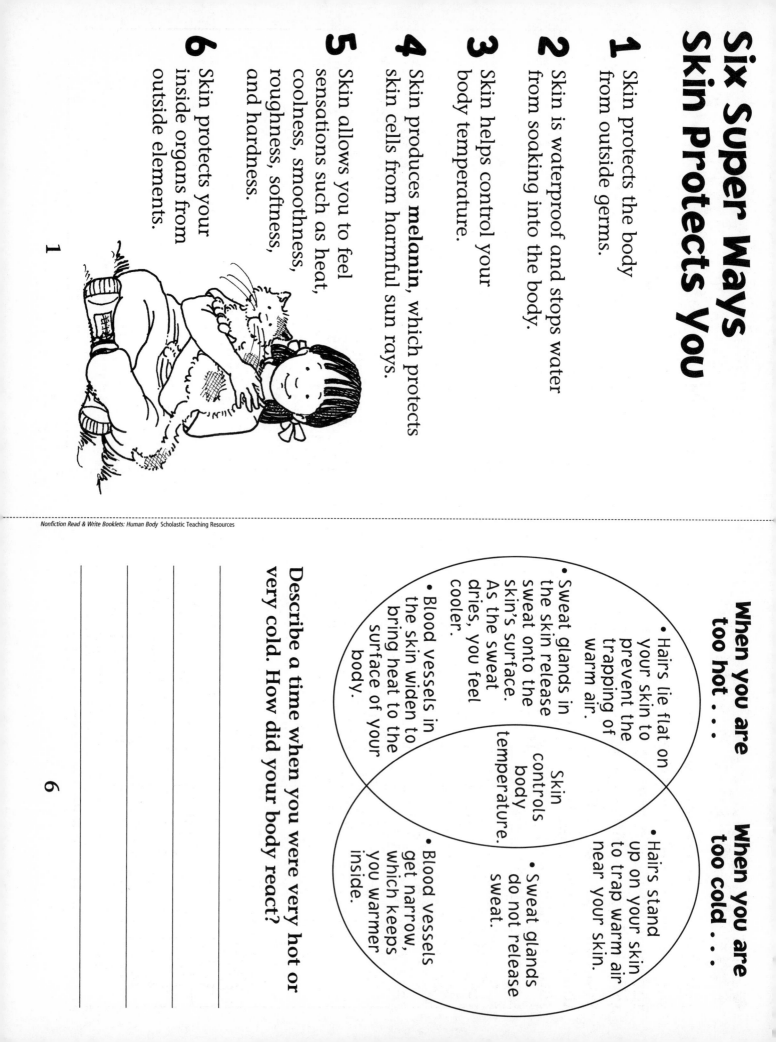

Nonfiction Read & Write Booklets: Human Body Scholastic Teaching Resources

When you are too hot . . .

- Hairs lie flat on your skin to prevent the trapping of warm air.

- Sweat glands in the skin release sweat onto the skin's surface. As the sweat dries, you feel cooler.

- Blood vessels in the skin widen to bring heat to the surface of your body.

Skin controls body temperature.

When you are too cold . . .

- Hairs stand up on your skin to trap warm air near your skin.

- Sweat glands do not release sweat.

- Blood vessels get narrow, which keeps you warmer inside.

Describe a time when you were very hot or very cold. How did your body react?

_____

_____

_____

_____

Were you surprised to learn about all the ways that skin protects you?

_____

Explain your answer.

_____

_____

_____

Look closely at the skin on your arm. What do you see? Draw a detailed picture showing what it looks like.

2

Temperature Control

Did you know that your body temperature stays at about 98.6 degrees Fahrenheit no matter what the air is like around you? If your body temperature gets too high or low, you could become sick. The skin is the organ that helps keep your body at about the same temperature.

98.6 °F

5

A Closer Look at Skin

The surface of the **epidermis layer** of skin is covered with dead skin cells. New skin cells are always replacing dead skin cells, which flake away.

The **dermis layer** of skin contains hair follicles, sweat glands, blood vessels, and sensory receptors.

The **fat layer** helps keep you warm.

Hairs start growing in the **hair follicles**. The hairs grow through the epidermis.

Sweat comes out of the **sweat pores** in the epidermis.

Sweat glands produce sweat, which helps keep the body cool.

Sensory receptors help you feel things that touch your skin.

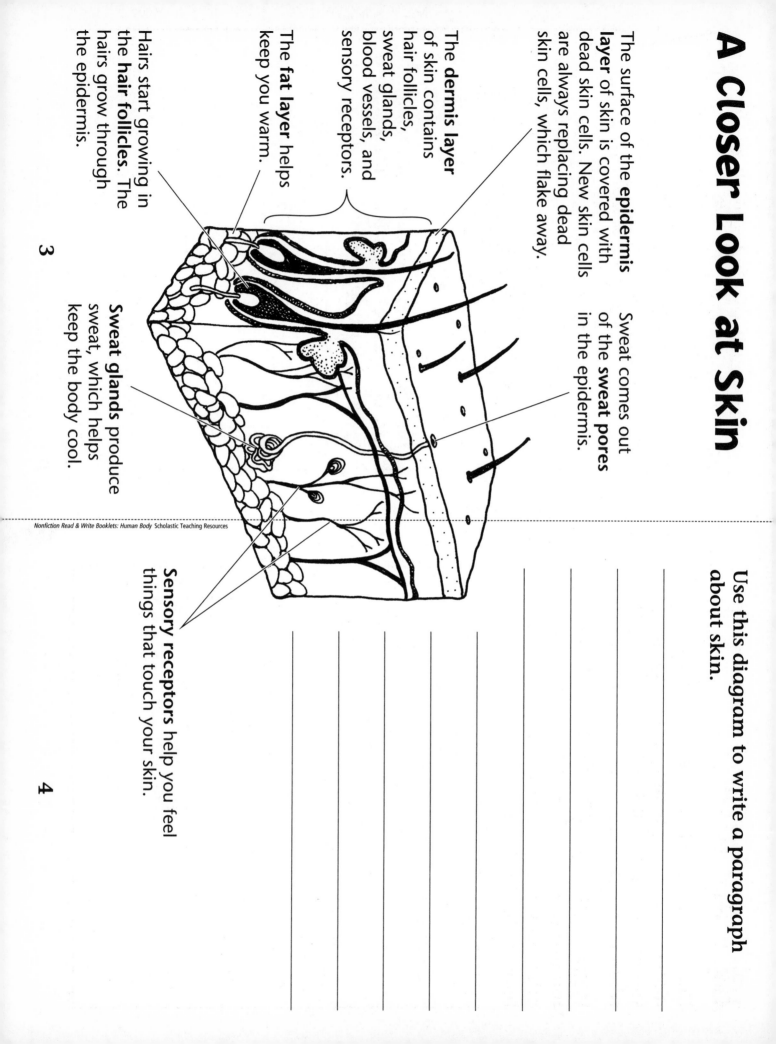

Nonfiction Read & Write Booklets: Human Body Scholastic Teaching Resources

3

Use this diagram to write a paragraph about skin.

_____

_____

_____

_____

_____

_____

_____

_____

_____

_____

_____

4

My Book About Staying Healthy

by _____

Hi, Doc!

Doctors are trained to give checkups and make sure our bodies are working as they should. They also help us get healthy again when we become sick.

Write a letter to a friend explaining why it's important to go to the doctor. Include some other tips about staying healthy that you learned in this book.

Dear _____,

_____

_____

_____

_____

_____

Sincerely,

_____

7

Five Ways to Stay Healthy

Here are five ways to give your body what it needs!

1. drinking water

2. eating healthy food

3. sleeping

4. exercising

5. bathing

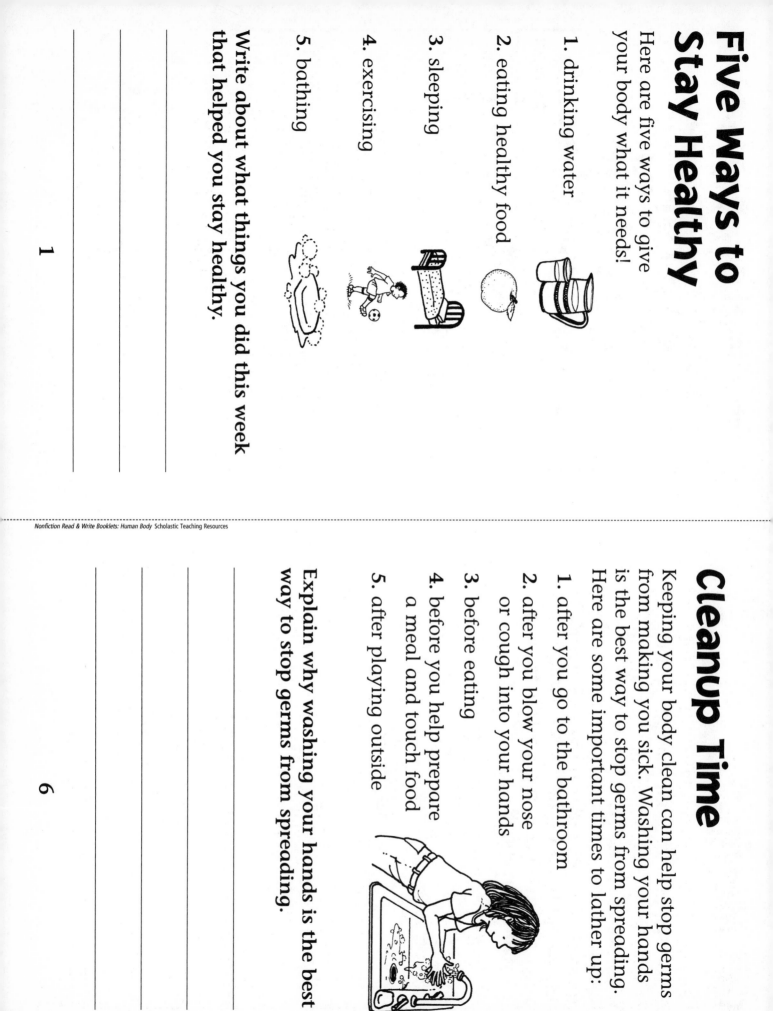

Write about what things you did this week that helped you stay healthy.

Cleanup Time

Keeping your body clean can help stop germs from making you sick. Washing your hands is the best way to stop germs from spreading. Here are some important times to lather up:

1. after you go to the bathroom

2. after you blow your nose or cough into your hands

3. before eating

4. before you help prepare a meal and touch food

5. after playing outside

Explain why washing your hands is the best way to stop germs from spreading.

More Water, Please!

Your body needs water to live and work well. If your body does not get enough water, it becomes **dehydrated**. This condition can be dangerous.

How to Tell if You Are Dehydrated

1. You feel very thirsty.

2. You feel very tired even if you've been getting enough sleep.

3. You go to the bathroom once or twice a day instead of five or six times a day.

How to Keep From Getting Dehydrated

1. Drink six to eight glasses of water each day.

2. You can also get lots of water from foods such as grapes, oranges, lettuce, and celery.

3. If you play outside on a hot day, stop for water breaks and for rest in the shade.

2

Nonfiction Read & Write Booklets: Human Body Scholastic Teaching Resources

Get Moving!

Did you know that you probably exercise without even knowing it? Just being active is a way to exercise. That means that every time you play a sport, jump rope, ride a bike, play tag, play hopscotch, or build a snowman you are exercising. Being active helps your body stay strong. Here's how:

exercise
- makes your muscles stronger
- makes you feel energized
- makes your heart stronger
- makes you flexible

What are your favorite ways to be active?

_____

_____

_____

5

Please Pass the Peas

Food gives your body energy. The healthier the food you eat, the more energy you will have. A balanced diet includes foods from each group.

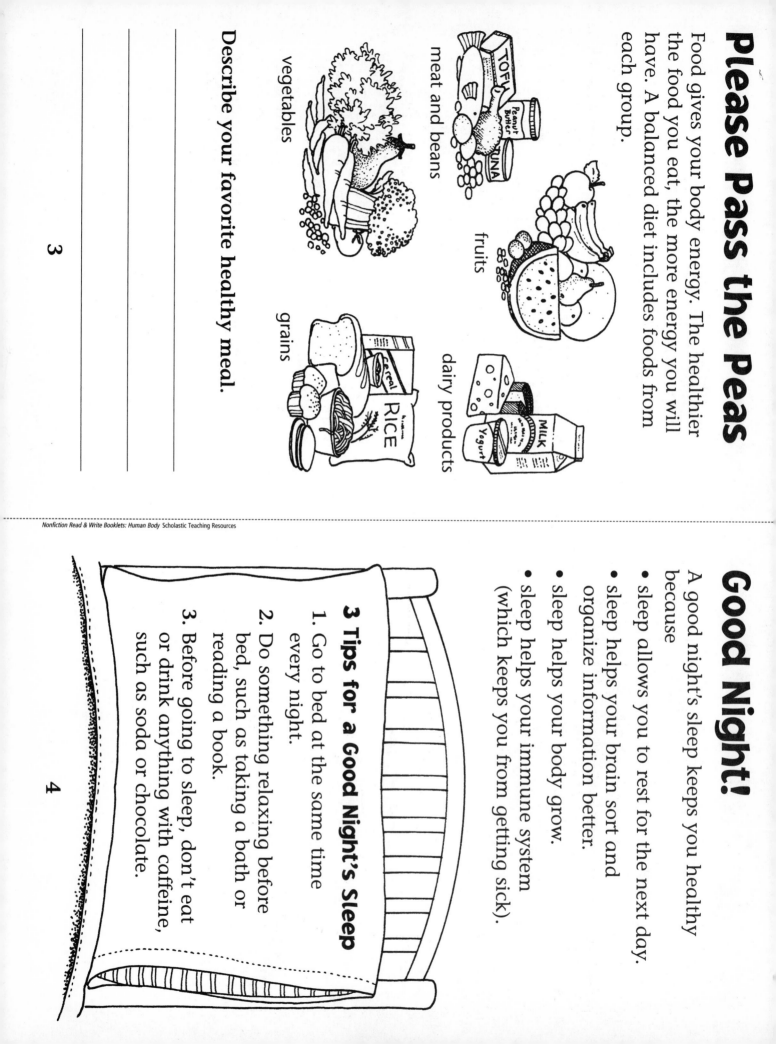

meat and beans

vegetables

fruits

grains

dairy products

Describe your favorite healthy meal.

_____

_____

_____

3

Good Night!

A good night's sleep keeps you healthy because

• sleep allows you to rest for the next day.

• sleep helps your brain sort and organize information better.

• sleep helps your body grow.

• sleep helps your immune system (which keeps you from getting sick).

3 Tips for a Good Night's Sleep

1. Go to bed at the same time every night.

2. Do something relaxing before bed, such as taking a bath or reading a book.

3. Before going to sleep, don't eat or drink anything with caffeine, such as soda or chocolate.

4

Senses at Work

Think about an activity that you love to do, such as drawing, riding your bike, or playing a sport. Draw a picture that shows you doing that activity. Then describe how you use your senses when you do the activity. How many senses do you use?

7

My Book About the Five Senses

by _____

The Five Senses

Our senses allow us to see our friends, hear a guitar, smell cookies baking, taste a crisp apple, and feel a warm breeze. What makes this possible? Our sense organs: the eyes, ears, nose, tongue, and skin. Each sense organ sends messages about the world to our brain with special nerve cells called receptors.

Where are the receptors for each sense?

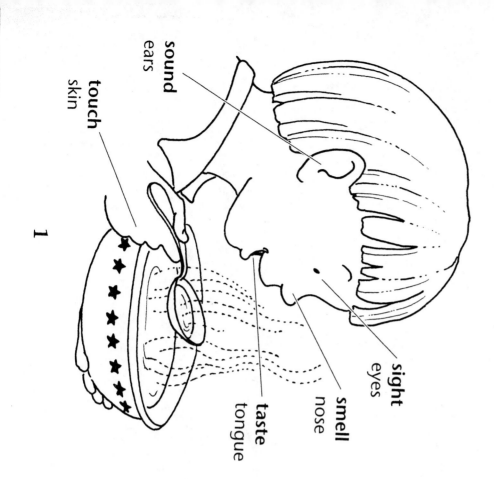

sight
eyes

smell
nose

taste
tongue

sound
ears

touch
skin

1

Taste buds are not the tiny bumps you can see on your tongue. Those are called **papillae**. Taste buds are mostly found on the papillae but are too small to see. The tongue has about 10,000 taste buds.

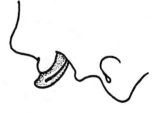

Skin is the largest organ.

Which fact or facts did you find most interesting? Why?

6

Did You Know . . . ?

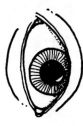

Most of the eyeball is hidden in your skull.

As you get older, your sense of smell gets worse.

The ear cleans itself. Sticky wax inside the ear traps dirt. When the wax dries up, it moves to the outside of your ear and falls out. Your ear is always making more wax.

5

Nonfiction Read & Write Booklets: Human Body Scholastic Teaching Resources

---

I use my eyes to . . .

I use my ears to . . .

I use my nose to . . .

I use my tongue to . . .

I use my skin to . . .

2

How the senses work

sight	You see something when light bounces off an object and back to your eyes. Receptors react to the light and send an image to the brain.
hearing	You hear a sound when vibrations in the air travel deep into your ear. The vibrations cause the liquid in the inner ear to move, which makes tiny hairs move. This movement sends signals to the brain.
smell	You smell something when tiny particles in the air enter your nose. Deep in the nose, receptors send a message about the odor to the brain.
taste	You taste when food dissolved in saliva passes over the taste buds on your tongue. Receptors send messages about the taste to the brain.
touch	You have receptors in the skin that detect sensations such as temperature, pain, and pressure. These receptors send messages to the brain about what you feel.

3

Nonfiction Read & Write Booklets: Human Body Scholastic Teaching Resources

Does the brain play a small role or big role in how you see, hear, smell, taste, and feel things?

_____

_____

Explain your answer.

_____

_____

_____

_____

_____

_____

_____

_____

4

Caring for Your Teeth

1. Brush your teeth at least twice a day.
2. Floss to remove food that's stuck between your teeth.
3. Eat healthy foods.
4. Go to the dentist for checkups and cleanings.

Look at your smile in the mirror. Then draw a picture of your smile in the mirror below.

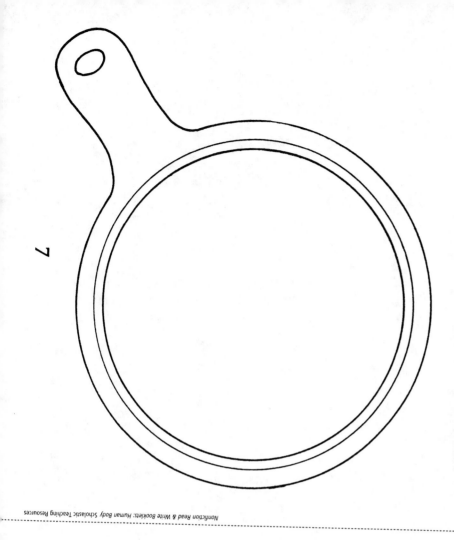

7

Nonfiction Read & Write Booklets: Human Body Scholastic Teaching Resources

My Book About Teeth

by _____

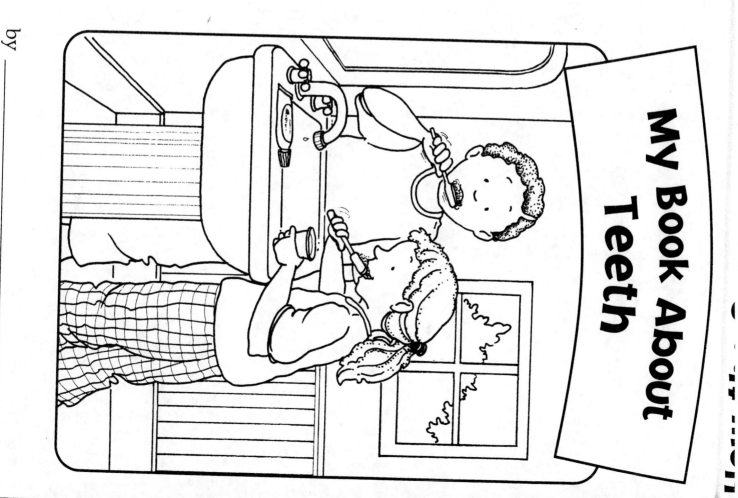

Thank you, Teeth!

What do your teeth do? Read the web below to find out.

They help give your face its shape.

They help you bite and chew food.

Teeth

They help you say certain sounds (like the **th** sound in **teeth**).

Why do we have different kinds of teeth?

_____

_____

Explain why it would be difficult to eat a piece of pizza without your incisors.

_____

_____

_____

_____

_____

Nonfiction Read & Write Booklets: Human Body Scholastic Teaching Resources

Different Teeth for Different Jobs

TYPES OF PERMANENT TEETH

incisors	These teeth have sharp, flat ends for slicing through food when you bite.
canines	These sharp, pointy teeth help you grip and tear food.
premolars	Premolars have ridges for crushing and grinding food.
molars	Molars are the strongest teeth. They are wider and stronger and have more ridges than premolars.

Your Changing Mouth

Babies are born without teeth. By six or seven months, **primary teeth** (also called baby teeth) begin to come in. All 20 baby teeth are in by age 3.

Between ages 5 and 7, the baby teeth begin to fall out, one by one. The baby teeth are pushed out of the way by your **permanent teeth.**

By about age 14, you will have your full set of permanent teeth—28 in all.

Beginning at age 16, four **wisdom teeth** come in. These are the teeth in the very back of your mouth.

How many teeth have you lost so far?

_____

What's in a Tooth?

Enamel is a hard and shiny substance that covers the crown and protects the tooth.

Dentin is a hard material that makes up much of the tooth. It protects the pulp in the center of the tooth.

The **crown** is the part of the tooth you can see above the gum.

The **pulp** is where the nerve endings and blood vessels are found.

The **root** is the part of the tooth below the gum.

Nerves send messages to the brain about what the tooth is feeling.

Blood vessels bring nutrients to the tooth and keep it healthy.

The **jawbone** is where the root of the tooth is held in place.

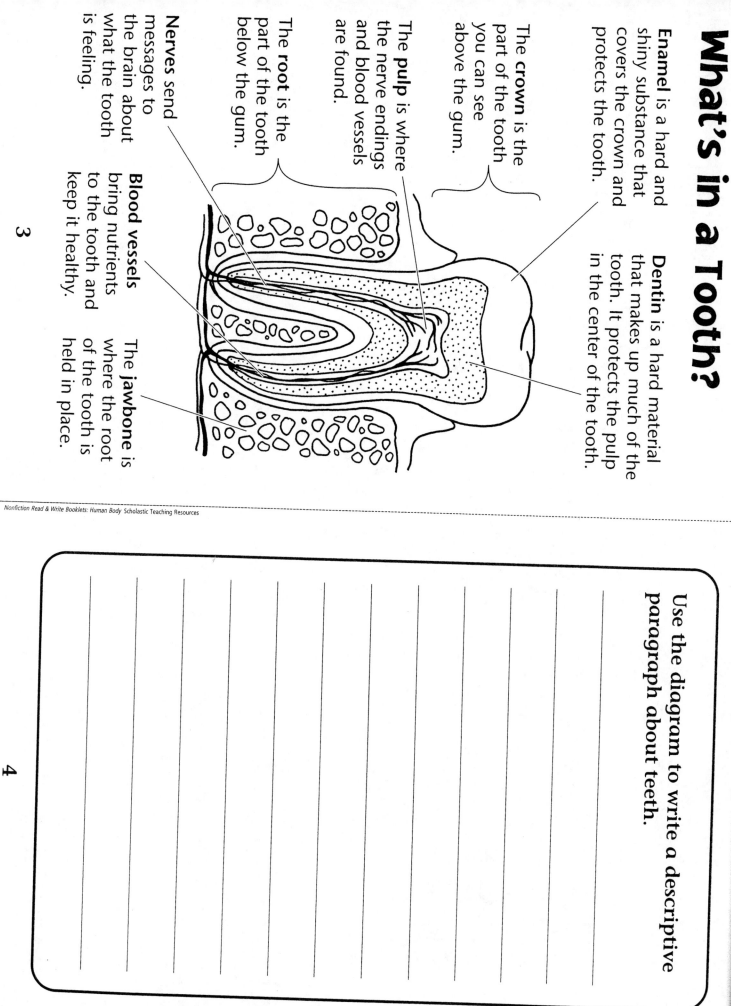

3

Use the diagram to write a descriptive **paragraph about teeth.**

4

Super Sunscreen

The best way to care for your skin is to wear sunscreen. Sunscreen actually helps block the harmful rays of the sun from burning and damaging your skin.

Imagine you created a new brand of sunscreen. Give it a name and write an advertisement for your sunscreen. Describe its color, smell, and protective powers. Then draw a label for the bottle.

7

My Book About Skin

by _____

Six Super Ways
Skin Protects You

1 Skin protects the body from outside germs.

2 Skin is waterproof and stops water from soaking into the body.

3 Skin helps control your body temperature.

4 Skin produces **melanin**, which protects skin cells from harmful sun rays.

5 Skin allows you to feel sensations such as heat, coolness, smoothness, roughness, softness, and hardness.

6 Skin protects your inside organs from outside elements.

Nonfiction Read & Write Booklets: Human Body Scholastic Teaching Resources

When you are too hot . . . . When you are too cold . . . .

- Hairs lie flat on your skin to prevent the trapping of warm air.

- Sweat glands in the skin release sweat onto the skin's surface. As the sweat dries, you feel cooler.

- Blood vessels in the skin widen to bring heat to the surface of your body.

Skin controls body temperature.

- Hairs stand up on your skin to trap warm air near your skin.

- Sweat glands do not release sweat.

- Blood vessels get narrow, which keeps you warmer inside.

Describe a time when you were very hot or very cold. How did your body react?

_____

_____

_____

_____

_____

Temperature Control

Did you know that your body temperature stays at about 98.6 degrees Fahrenheit no matter what the air is like around you? If your body temperature gets too high or low, you could become sick. The skin is the organ that helps keep your body at about the same temperature.

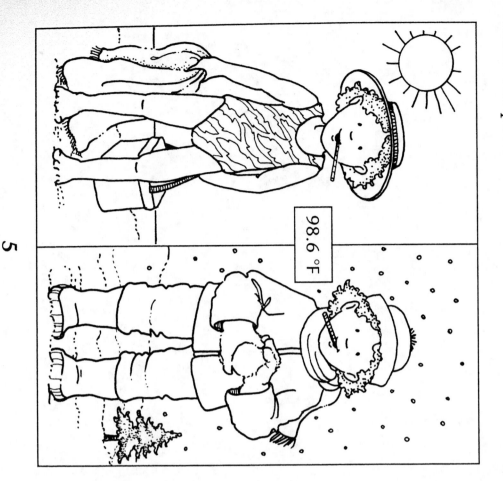

98.6 °F

Were you surprised to learn about all the ways that skin protects you?

Explain your answer.

Look closely at the skin on your arm. What do you see? Draw a detailed picture showing what it looks like.

A Closer Look at Skin

The surface of the **epidermis layer** of skin is covered with dead skin cells. New skin cells are always replacing dead skin cells, which flake away.

The **dermis layer** of skin contains hair follicles, sweat glands, blood vessels, and sensory receptors.

The **fat layer** helps keep you warm.

Hairs start growing in the **hair follicles.** The hairs grow through the epidermis.

3

Sweat comes out of the **sweat pores** in the epidermis.

Sweat glands produce sweat, which helps keep the body cool.

Sensory receptors help you feel things that touch your skin.

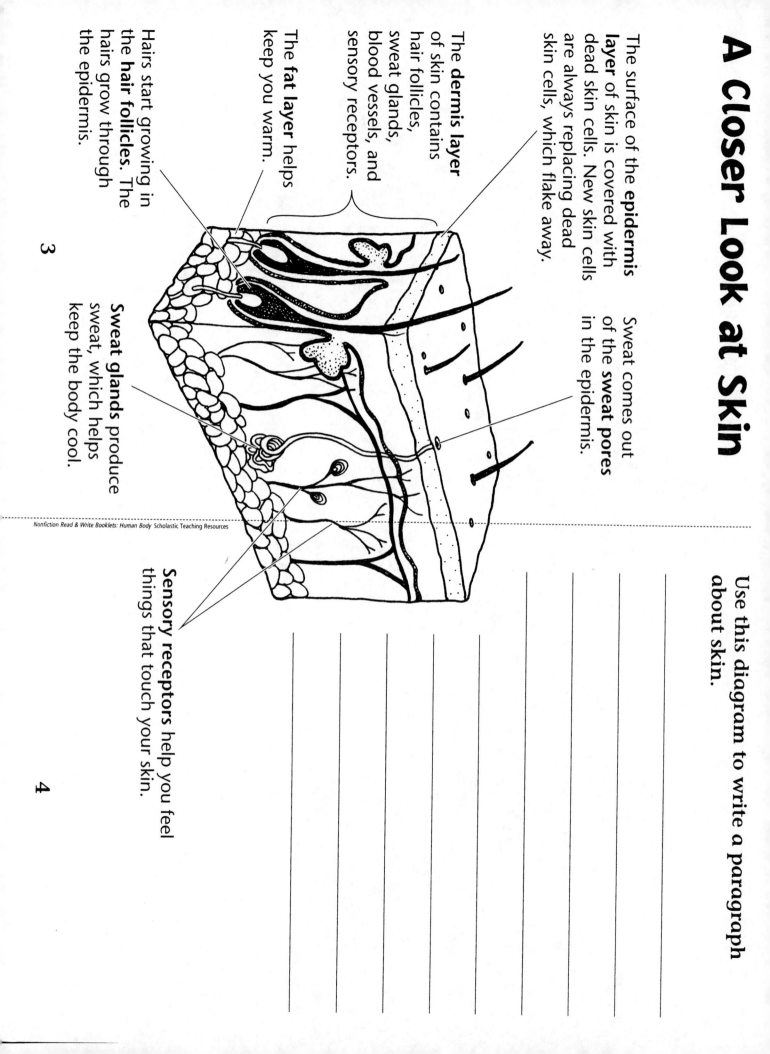

Use this diagram to write a paragraph about skin.

4

Hi, Doc!

Doctors are trained to give checkups and make sure our bodies are working as they should. They also help us get healthy again when we become sick.

Write a letter to a friend explaining why it's important to go to the doctor. Include some other tips about staying healthy that you learned in this book.

Dear _____,

_____
_____
_____
_____
_____

Sincerely,

_____

7

Nonfiction Read & Write Booklets: Human Body Scholastic Teaching Resources

My Book About Staying Healthy

by _____

Five Ways to Stay Healthy

Here are five ways to give your body what it needs!

1. drinking water

2. eating healthy food

3. sleeping

4. exercising

5. bathing

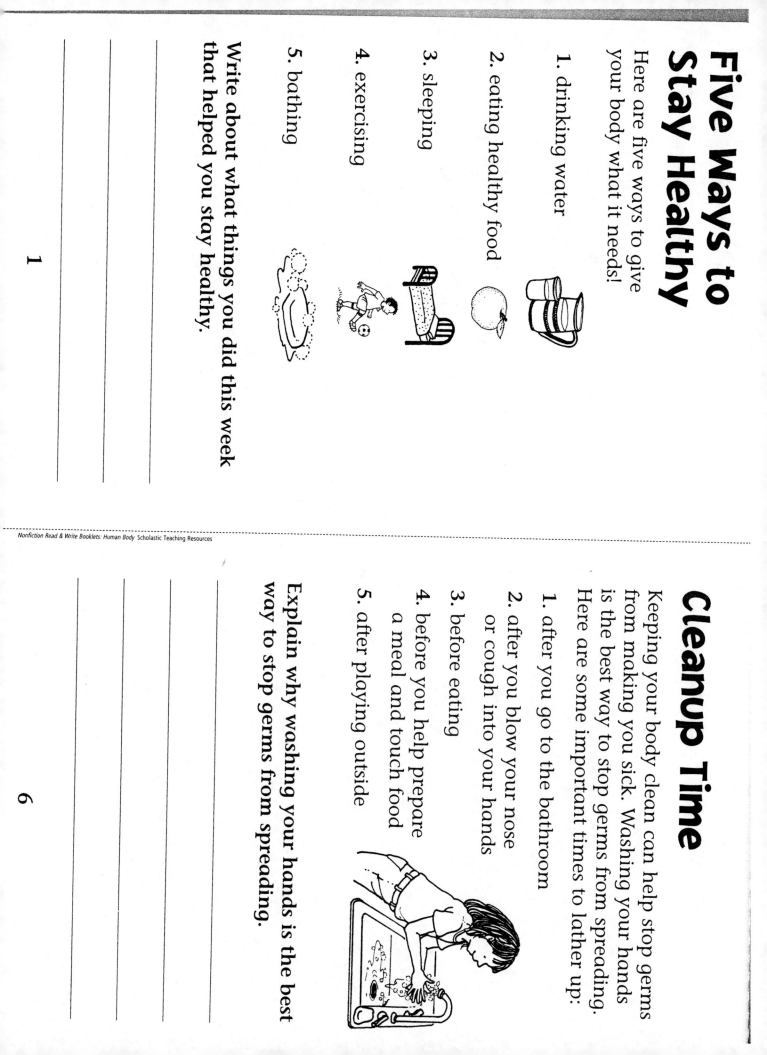

Write about what things you did this week that helped you stay healthy.

_____

_____

_____

Nonfiction Read & Write Booklets: Human Body Scholastic Teaching Resources

---

Cleanup Time

Keeping your body clean can help stop germs from making you sick. Washing your hands is the best way to stop germs from spreading. Here are some important times to lather up:

1. after you go to the bathroom

2. after you blow your nose or cough into your hands

3. before eating

4. before you help prepare a meal and touch food

5. after playing outside

Explain why washing your hands is the best way to stop germs from spreading.

_____

_____

_____

Get Moving!

Did you know that you probably exercise without even knowing it? Just being active is a way to exercise. That means that every time you play a sport, jump rope, ride a bike, play tag, play hopscotch, or build a snowman you are exercising. Being active helps your body stay strong. Here's how:

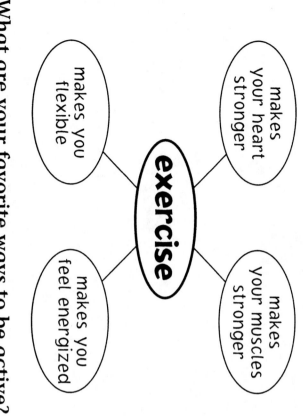

makes your heart stronger

exercise

makes your muscles stronger

makes you flexible

makes you feel energized

What are your favorite ways to be active?

Nonfiction Read & Write Booklets: Human Body Scholastic Teaching Resources

---

More Water, Please!

Your body needs water to live and work well. If your body does not get enough water, it becomes dehydrated. This condition can be dangerous.

How to Tell if You Are Dehydrated

1. You feel very thirsty.

2. You feel very tired even if you've been getting enough sleep.

3. You go to the bathroom once or twice a day instead of five or six times a day.

How to Keep From Getting Dehydrated

1. Drink six to eight glasses of water each day.

2. You can also get lots of water from foods such as grapes, oranges, lettuce, and celery.

3. If you play outside on a hot day, stop for water breaks and for rest in the shade.

Please Pass the Peas

Food gives your body energy. The healthier the food you eat, the more energy you will have. A balanced diet includes foods from each group.

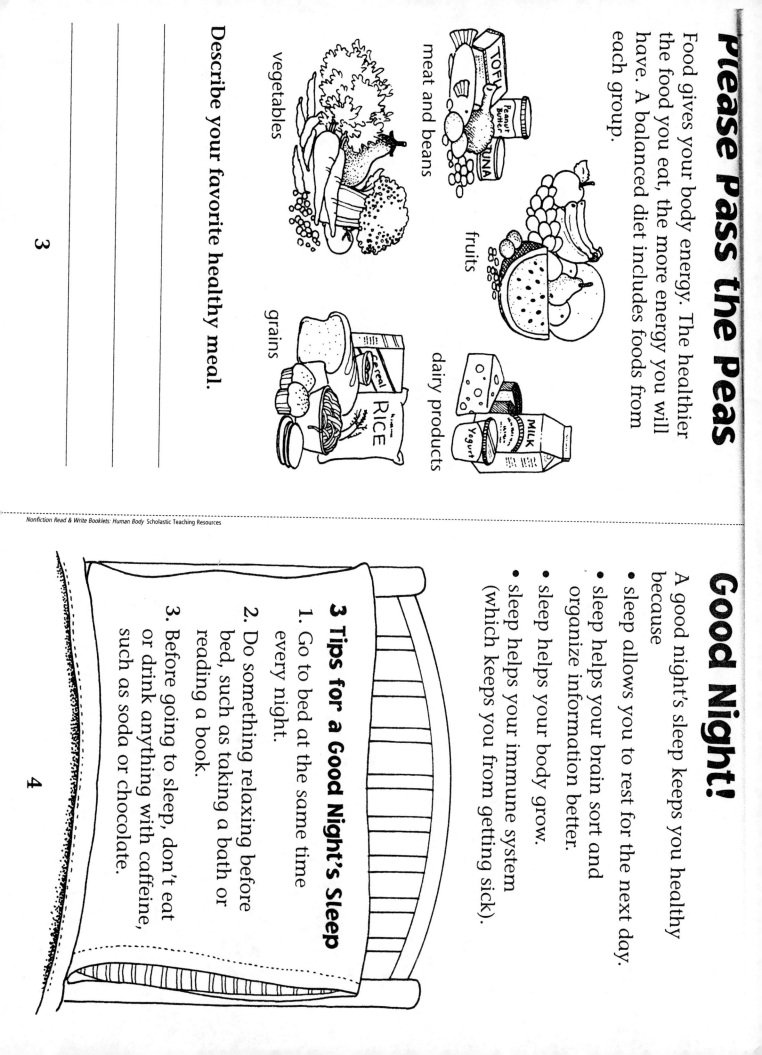

meat and beans

fruits

vegetables

dairy products

grains

Describe your favorite healthy meal.

_____

_____

_____

Nonfiction Read & Write Booklets: Human Body Scholastic Teaching Resources

Good Night!

A good night's sleep keeps you healthy because

- sleep allows you to rest for the next day.
- sleep helps your brain sort and organize information better.
- sleep helps your body grow.
- sleep helps your immune system (which keeps you from getting sick).

3 Tips for a Good Night's Sleep

1. Go to bed at the same time every night.
2. Do something relaxing before bed, such as taking a bath or reading a book.
3. Before going to sleep, don't eat or drink anything with caffeine, such as soda or chocolate.